2

Does the Exchange Rate Regime Matter for Inflation and Growth?

Atish R. Ghosh
Ann-Marie Gulde
Jonathan D. Ostry
Holger Wolf

International Monetary Fund
Washington, D.C.

ISBN: 1-55775-614-7

Published September 1996

To order IMF publications, please contact:

International Monetary Fund, Publication Services
700 19th Street, N.W., Washington, D.C. 20431, U.S.A.
Tel.: (202) 623-7430   Telefax: (202) 623-7201
Internet: publications@imf.org

Preface

The Economic Issues series was inaugurated in September 1996. Its aim is to make some of the economic research being produced in the International Monetary Fund on topical issues accessible to a broad readership of nonspecialists. The raw material of the series is drawn mainly from IMF Working Papers, technical papers produced by Fund staff members and visiting scholars, as well as from policy-related research papers. This material is refined for the general readership by editing and partial redrafting.

The following paper draws on material originally contained in IMF Working Paper 95/121, "Does the Nominal Exchange Rate Regime Matter?" by Atish R. Ghosh, Anne-Marie Gulde, Johathan D. Ostry, and Holger Wolf. David D. Driscoll of the Fund's External Relations Department provided editorial assistance. Readers interested in the original Working Paper may purchase a copy from IMF Publication Services.

Does the Exchange Rate Regime Matter for Inflation and Growth?

Although the theoretical relationships are ambiguous, evidence suggests a strong link between the choice of the exchange rate regime and macroeconomic performance. Adopting a pegged exchange rate can lead to lower inflation, but also to slower productivity growth.

Few questions in international economics have aroused more debate than the choice of exchange rate regime. Should a country fix the exchange rate or allow it to float? And if pegged, to a single "hard" currency or a basket of currencies? Economic literature pullulates with models, theories, and propositions. Yet little consensus has emerged about how exchange rate regimes affect common macroeconomic targets, such as inflation and growth. At a theoretical level, it is difficult to establish unambiguous relationships because of the many ways in which exchange rates can influence—and be influenced by—other macroeconomic variables. Likewise, empirical studies typically find no clear link between the exchange rate regime and macroeconomic performance.

This paper seeks to identify how various exchange rate regimes influence inflation and growth. It goes beyond previous studies in three important respects. First, it uses more comprehensive data—comprising all IMF members from 1960–90. Second, it classifies exchange rate regimes in more detail than the traditional dichotomy between fixed and floating exchange rates. Third, it distinguishes between the central banks' declared exchange rate regimes and the behavior of the exchange rates in practice.

There is indeed a strong link between fixed exchange rates and low inflation. This results from a *discipline* effect (the political costs of abandoning the peg induce tighter policies) and a *confidence effect* (greater confidence leads to a greater willingness to hold domestic currency rather than goods or foreign currencies). In part, low inflation is associated with fixed exchange rates because countries with low inflation are better able to maintain an exchange rate peg. But there is also evidence of causality in the other direction: countries that choose fixed exchange rates achieve lower inflation.

There is also a link, albeit weaker, between the exchange rate regime and the growth of output. To the extent that fixing the exchange rate engenders greater policy confidence, it can foster higher investment. Conversely, a fixed rate, if set at the "wrong" level, can result in a misallocation of resources. In our data, countries that maintained pegged exchange rates did indeed have higher investment. But productivity grew more slowly than in countries with floating exchange rates. Overall, per capita growth was slightly lower in countries with pegged exchange rates.

This paper begins with a brief discussion of difficulties encountered in classifying exchange rate regimes. It then shows how alternative regimes affect inflation and growth. A few observations conclude the essay.

Classifying Regimes

Beyond the traditional fixed-floating dichotomy lies a spectrum of exchange rate regimes. The de facto behavior of an exchange rate, moreover, may diverge from its de jure classification.

While it is customary to speak of fixed and floating exchange rates, regimes actually span a continuum, ranging from pegs to target zones, to floats with heavy, light, or no intervention. The traditional dichotomy can mask important differences among regimes. Accordingly, this analysis uses a three-way classification: pegged, intermediate (i.e., floating rates, but within a predetermined range), and floating.

Regimes can be classified according to either the publicly stated commitment of the central bank (a *de jure* classification) or the observed behavior of the exchange rate (a *de facto* classification). Neither method is entirely satisfactory. A country that claims to have a pegged exchange rate might in fact instigate frequent changes in parity. On the other hand, a country might experience very small exchange rate movements, even though the central bank has no obligation to maintain a parity. The approach taken here is to report results according to the stated intention of the central bank, but to supplement these results by categorizing the nonfloating regimes according to whether or not changes in parity were frequent. The *de jure* classification uses the IMF's *Annual Report on Exchange Arrangements and Exchange Restrictions*, while the *de facto* classification is based on a survey of IMF desk officers for each country. The data are taken from the World Economic Outlook database. In all, observations of GDP growth and consumer price inflation cover 145 countries and 30 years.

Inflation

Pegging the exchange rate can lower inflation by inducing greater policy discipline and instilling greater confidence in the currency. Empirically, both effects are important.

Policymakers have long maintained that a pegged exchange rate can be an anti-inflationary tool. Two reasons are typically cited. A pegged exchange rate provides a highly visible commitment and thus raises the political costs of loose monetary and fiscal policies.

To the extent that the peg is credible, there is a stronger readiness to hold domestic currency, which reduces the inflationary consequences of a *given* expansion in the money supply.

Inflation Performance

Inflation over our sample averaged 10 percent a year, with pronounced differences in various exchange rate regimes (Chart 1). Countries with pegged exchange rates had an average annual inflation rate of 8 percent, compared with 14 percent for intermediate regimes, and 16 percent for floating regimes.

The differences among regimes are starker for the lower-income countries, where the differential between pegged and floating rates was almost 10 percentage points. As might be expected, countries without capital controls tended to have lower inflation in general. Even for these countries, however, inflation was lower under pegged regimes compared with either intermediate or floating exchange rates.

Although inflation performance is generally better under pegged exchange rates, the last panel in Chart 1 illustrates an important caveat: mere declaration of a pegged exchange rate is insufficient to reap the full anti-inflationary benefits. Countries that changed their parity frequently—though notionally maintaining a pegged exchange rate—on average experienced 13 percent inflation. While this is still better than the performance under nonpegged exchange rates (17 percent), it is significantly worse than countries that maintained a stable parity (7 percent).

Since there was a preponderance of pegged exchange rate regimes in the 1960s—when inflation rates were low—the association between low inflation and pegged rates might be more an artifact of the general macroeconomic climate than a property of the regime itself. One way to purge the data of such effects is to measure inflation rates for each regime relative to the average inflation rate (across all regimes) in that year. Doing so, however, leaves the story largely unchanged: as Chart 1 shows, under pegged rates, inflation was 3 percentage points lower than under intermediate and 6 percentage points less than under floating regimes. Again, coun-

Chart 1. Inflation Performance
(In percent per year)

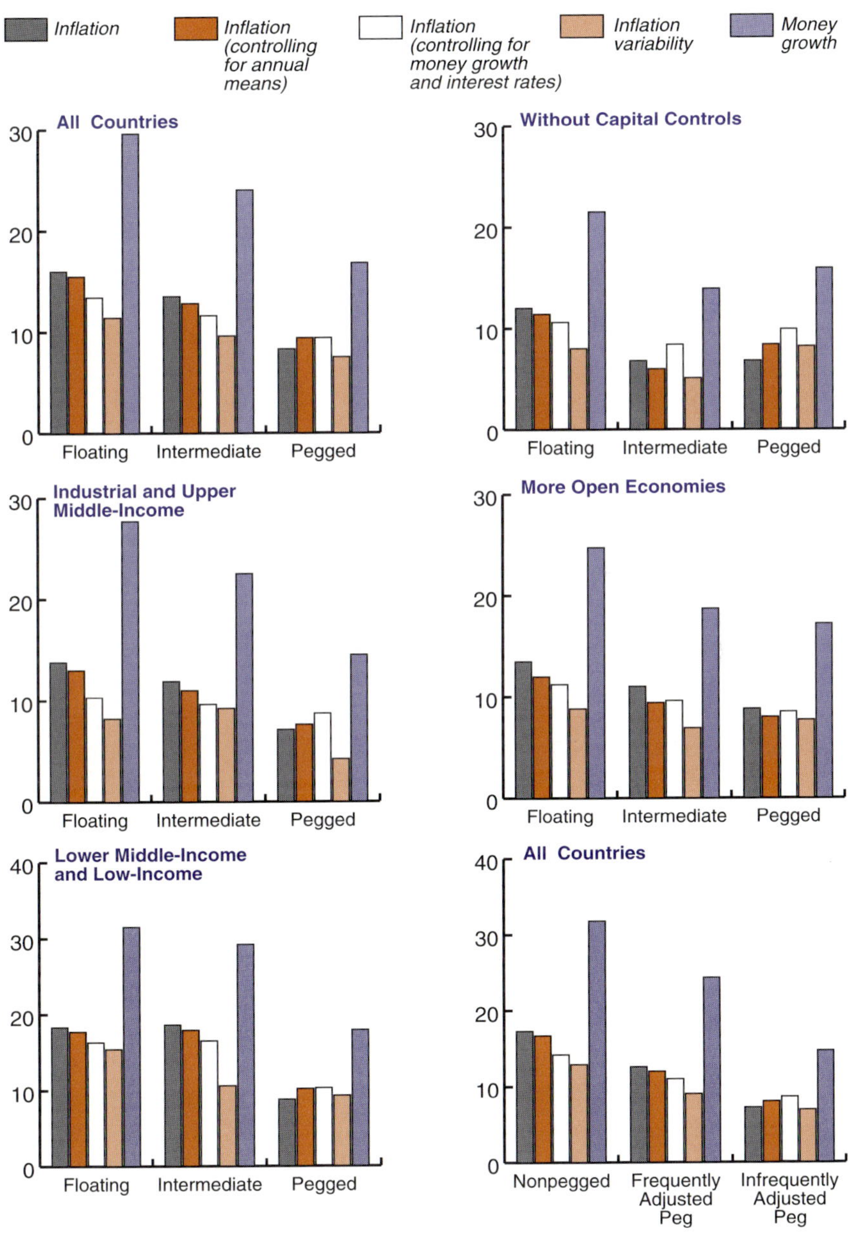

tries with only occasional changes in parity fared significantly better than those with frequent changes.

Explaining the Differences

What accounts for these results? They derive, in fact, from two separate effects. The first is discipline. Countries with pegged exchange rates have lower rates of growth in money supply, presumably because of the political costs of abandoning a peg. The growth of broad money (currency and deposits) averaged 17 percent a year under pegged exchange rates compared with almost 30 percent under floating regimes. This difference holds regardless of the income level of the country.

In addition, for a *given* growth rate of the money supply, higher money demand (the desire to hold money rather than spend it) will imply lower inflation. Pegged exchange rates, by enhancing confidence, can engender a greater demand for the domestic currency. This will be reflected in a lower velocity of circulation and a faster decline of domestic interest rates. In the extreme case of perfect credibility, domestic interest rates—even in countries with a history of high inflation—should fall immediately to the world level. Over the sample period, nominal interest rates have tended to rise, but the rate of increase for countries with floating rates was almost 6 percent, as against 2 percent for countries with pegged rates. It was actually highest for countries with intermediate regimes, where the growth rate of interest rates was almost 9 percent. A change in nominal interest rates is of importance because a fall in these rates will lead to a stronger demand for money. But the level of real interest rates (i.e., the nominal rates adjusted for inflation) also gives a direct measure of confidence. On average, the real interest rates were 0.2 percent a year under pegged regimes, 1.8 percent under intermediate regimes, and 2.3 percent under floating regimes.

For a variety of reasons—including interest rates that are set by the authorities rather than being determined by the market—the greater confidence that pegged exchanges can bring may not be fully reflected in the observed domestic interest rate. Nonetheless, it is possible to identify the "confidence effect" of various regimes by considering the residual inflation once the effects of money expansion, real growth, and domestic interest rates have been removed. A higher residual inflation implies lower confidence.

Do pegged rates lead to greater confidence? They do. Chart 1 shows the residual inflation rates. Countries with pegged exchange rates had inflation 2 percentage points lower than those with intermediate regimes, and 4 percentage points lower than those with floating regimes. This differential in favor of pegged rates is as large as 6 percentage points in the lower-income countries, but only 3 percentage points for countries without capital controls—perhaps because abjuring capital controls itself inspires confidence in the domestic currency.

Not only do countries with pegged exchange rates have lower inflation on average, they are also associated with lower inflation variability.

The Dog or the Tail?

Does pegging the exchange rate cause lower inflation? Or is it merely that countries with low inflation are better able to maintain a pegged exchange rate regime? Quite obviously, a country with reckless monetary policy will not be able to keep its exchange rate fixed for long. Part of the argument for pegged rates is precisely that they result in greater monetary discipline. But that still leaves the question of whether other variables—such as the degree of central bank independence—determine both a country's disposition toward low inflation and its ability to adopt a pegged exchange rate.

Econometric studies of this simultaneity between the choice of the exchange rate regime and inflation (using the same data) suggest that countries with low inflation do indeed have a greater proclivity toward pegged exchange rates. But they also show that, even allowing for this, pegged exchange rates lead to lower inflation.

Simpler, if less compelling, evidence comes from a comparison of countries that switched to a pegged exchange rate (from a floating regime) or vice versa. Relative to the year preceding the regime change, inflation was 0.6 percentage points lower one year after a switch to a fixed exchange rate regime, 0.5 percentage points lower after two years, and 0.5 percentage points lower after three years. Conversely, inflation was higher by 3 percentage points one year after a switch to a floating regime, 1.8 percentage points higher after two years, and 2.3 percentage points higher after three years.

A second piece of evidence comes from a comparison of countries with similar volatility in nominal effective exchange rates but different exchange rate regimes. Countries with pegged exchanges rates, of course, tend to exhibit lower effective exchange rate variability. But if the exchange rate *regime* matters for inflation, there should still be a difference between countries with pegged and floating exchange rates even after controlling for nominal exchange rate variability. It turns out that this is indeed the case. Controlling for nominal exchange rate variability, there remain significant differences in inflation in the various regimes. In other words, pegging the nominal exchange rate—which may instill greater confidence— has an effect on inflation beyond simply lowering nominal exchange rate variability.

Finally, it is worth checking that the results are not driven by contamination across regimes. For instance, it is possible for inflationary pressure to build up—but be held in check—during a period of pegged exchange rates and then explode into open inflation when a float is adopted. In such a case, the high inflation would be blamed on the floating regime, though it should more properly be attributed to the fixed exchange rate period. This suggests dropping the first year or two following a regime change from the data. Conversely, if a regime is not sustained, then it is debatable whether the macroeconomic performance under that regime should be attributed to it. The last couple of years prior to a regime change. ought also to be omitted. Neither modification alters the results. Dropping the first two years following a regime change lowers the differential in favor of pegged rates from 6.0 percentage points to 5.7 percentage points. Dropping the last two years of each regime lowers it to 5.8 percentage points.

Chart 2. Per Capita GDP Growth
(In percent per year)

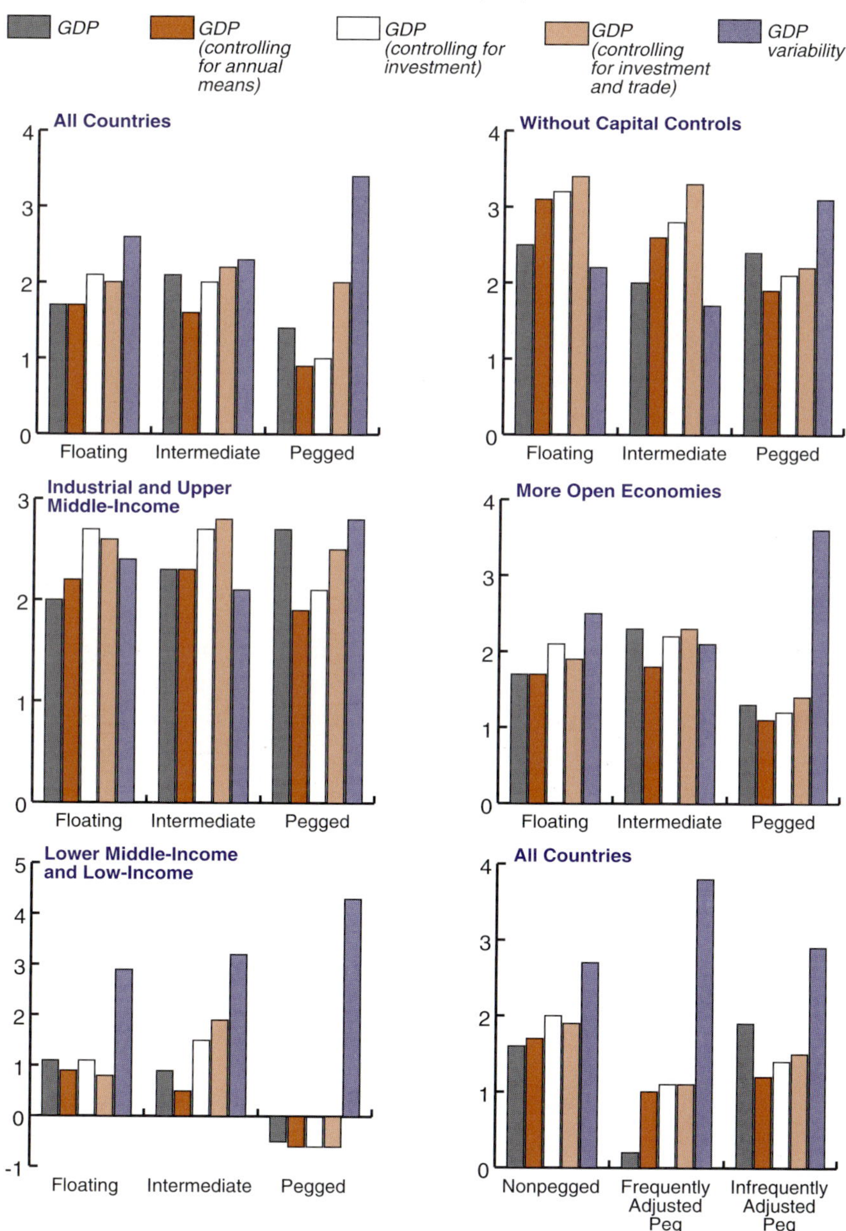

Growth

The exchange rate regime can influence economic growth through investment or increased productivity. Pegged regimes have higher investment; floating regimes have faster productivity growth. On net, per capita GDP growth was slightly faster under floating regimes.

Economic theory has relatively little to say about the effects of the nominal exchange rate regime on the growth of output. Typically, arguments focus on the impact on investment and international trade. Advocates argue that pegged exchange rates foster investment by reducing policy uncertainties and lowering real interest rates. But equally, by eliminating an important adjustment mechanism, fixed exchange rates can increase protectionist pressure, distort price signals in the economy, and prevent the efficient allocation of resources across sectors.

Growth Performance

Annual GDP growth per capita averaged 1.6 percent over our sample. Although differences exist across exchange rate regimes, these are generally less marked than the differences in inflation rates (Chart 2). Different samples, moreover, lead to varied conclusions about growth under fixed and floating exchange rates. Growth was actually fastest under the intermediate regimes, averaging more than 2 percent a year. It was 1.4 percent a year under pegged exchange rates and 1.7 percent under floating rates. This pattern emerges mainly because of the lower middle-income and low-income countries; growth was somewhat higher under pegged rates for the industrial and upper middle-income countries.

Just as inflation was generally lower in the 1960s, growth rates tended to be higher. Controlling for this widens the differential in favor of floating exchange rates to 0.8 percent over all countries, and as much as 1.5 percent for the lower-income countries.

By definition, economic growth can be explained by the use of more capital and labor (the factors of production) or by residual productivity growth. This productivity growth reflects both technological progress and—perhaps more important—changes in the economic efficiency with which capital and labor are used.

Investment rates were highest under pegged exchange rates—by as much as 2 percentage points of GDP—with the largest difference for the industrial and upper middle-income countries and almost none for the lower-income countries. With higher investment rates and lower output growth, productivity increases must have been smaller under fixed exchange rates.

Part of the higher productivity growth under floating rates is reflected in faster growth of external trade. Trade growth (measured as the sum of export growth and import growth) is almost 3 percentage points higher under floating rates. The lower-income countries—where real exchange rate misalignments under fixed rates have been more common—show an even larger difference in trade growth between pegged and floating exchange rates.

While not overwhelming, the evidence suggests that fixing the nominal exchange rate can prevent relative prices (including, perhaps, real wages) from adjusting. This lowers economic efficiency. Part, though not all, of this lower productivity growth is offset by higher investment under pegged exchange rates. A comparison of countries that switched regimes shows that a move to floating exchange rates results in an increase of GDP growth of 0.3 percentage points one year after the switch and of more than 1 percentage point three years after the switch. One manifestation of the rigidities that pegged exchange rates can engender is the higher volatility of GDP growth and of employment. As the last rows of Charts 7–12 indicate, GDP growth was more volatile under pegged exchange rates, as was employment.

Conclusions

Does the exchange rate regime matter for macroeconomic performance? The experience of IMF member countries since the 1960s suggests that it does.

The strongest results concern inflation. Pegged exchange rates are associated with significantly better inflation performance (lower inflation and less variability), and there is at least some evidence of a causal relationship. There is, however, an important caveat. Countries that have frequent parity changes—while notionally maintaining a peg—are unlikely to reap the full anti-inflationary benefits of a fixed exchange rate regime.

The choice of exchange rate regime also has implications for economic growth. Pegged rates are associated with higher investment. But they are also correlated with slower productivity growth. On net, output growth is slightly lower under pegged exchange rates. The inability to use the nominal exchange rate as an adjustment mechanism, moreover, results in greater variability of growth and employment.

Ultimately, the exchange rate regime is but one facet of a country's overall macroeconomic policy. No regime is likely to serve all countries at all times. Countries facing disinflation may find pegging the exchange rate an important tool. But where growth has been sluggish, and real exchange rate misalignments common, a more flexible regime might be called for. The choice, like the trade-off, is the country's own.

Bibliography

There is a vast literature on the link between the exchange rate regime and macroeconomic performance. The following provide useful surveys.

Argy, Victor, "The Choice of Exchange Rate Regime for a Smaller Economy: A Survey of Some Key Issues," in *Choosing an Exchange Rate Regime*, ed. by Victor Argy and Paul De Grauwe (Washington: International Monetary Fund, 1990).

Barth, Richard, and Chorng-Huey Wong (eds.), *Approaches to Exchange Rate Policy* (Washington: International Monetary Fund, 1994).

Baxter, Marianne, and Alan C. Stockman, *Business Cycles and the Exchange Rate System: Some Internal Evidence* (Cambridge, Massachusetts: National Bureau of Economic Research, 1988).

Crockett, Andrew, and Morris Goldstein, "Inflation Under Fixed and Flexible Exchange Rates," International Monetary Fund, *Staff Papers*, Vol. 23 (November 1976), pp. 509–44.

Frenkel, Jacob, Morris Goldstein, and Paul Masson, *Characteristics of a Successful Exchange Rate System*, Occasional Paper 82 (Washington: International Monetary Fund, 1991).

Friedman, Milton, "The Case For Flexible Exchange Rates," in *Essays in Positive Economics* (Chicago: University of Chicago Press, 1953).

Ghosh, Atish, Anne-Marie Gulde, Jonathan Ostry, and Holger Wolf, "Does the Nominal Exchange Rate Regime Matter?" IMF Working Paper 95/121 (December 1995).

Guitián, Manuel, "The Choice of an Exchange Rate Regime," in *Approaches to Exchange Rate Policy*, ed. by Richard Barth and Chorng-Huey Wong (Washington: International Monetary Fund, 1994).

Krugman, Paul, *Exchange Rate Instability* (Cambridge, Massachusetts: MIT Press, 1989).

Mussa, Michael, "Nominal Exchange Rate Regimes and the Behavior of Real Exchange Rates, Evidence and Implications," in *Real Business Cycles, Real Exchange Rates, and Actual Policies*, ed. by Karl Brunner and Alan Meltzer (Amsterdam: North-Holland, 1986).

Nurkse, Ragnar, *International Currency Experience* (Geneva: League of Nations, 1944).

Obstfeld, Maurice, "Floating Exchange Rates: Experience and Prospects," *Brookings Papers on Economic Activity: 2* (1985), pp. 369–450.

Quirk, Peter, "Fixed or Floating Exchange Regimes: Does It Matter For Inflation?" IMF Working Paper 94/134 (December 1994).

Williamson, John, "A Survey of the Literature on the Optimal Peg," *Journal of Development Economics*, Vol. 2 (August 1982), pp. 39–61.